Stop Smoking

Breaking Free: All Inclusive Help For Giving Up Smoking
And Taking Back Your Health And Well-being

(You Can Give Up Smoking By Using These Tips)

Robert Edlinger

TABLE OF CONTENT

The Rationale Behind Quitting Smoking 1

Making The Choice To Give Up Smoking 5

The Approach I've Taken To Stop 12

What Smoking May Do To Your Conceptual Framework And Ability To Coexist Sexually. 20

Benefits And Drawbacks Of Smoking 38

What You Get From Smoking 50

Smoking And Suffering The Repercussions 63

Using Self-Awareness And Mindfulness To Help You Stop Smoking 74

Additional Easy Methods To Help You Beat The Need For Nicotine 82

The Toughest Way To Give Up: Health Issues 98

Take Notes From Past Attempts 117

The Rationale Behind Quitting Smoking

Some People Who Are Trying To Quit Smoking After Realizing How Much It Has Harmed Their Relationships With Friends And Family Will Find It Challenging Since Leaving Or Reducing Tobacco Usage Results In Withdrawal Symptoms From Nicotine, Which Include Both Physical And Psychological Symptoms. Physically, Your Body Will Respond To The Lack Of Nicotine Or Nicotine-Related Material; Psychologically, You Are Moving Toward Quitting With A Behavioral Act That Promotes A Significant Shift In Habit. If You Have Always Smoked, Your Family And Friends May Have Encouraged You To Give It Up. You Are Undoubtedly Also Aware That Smoking Contributes To A Number Of Chronic Illnesses, Such As Heart Disease, Cancer, Stroke, Chronic Bronchitis, And Others, That Can Be Fatal. It's Not Exactly The Best Reason

To Give Up To Know That There Are Long-Term Concerns That Could Manifest Decades From Now. Some Smokers Find That Tiny, Fascinating Things—Like The Looks On People's Faces When They Find Out They Smoke, The Stains On Their Teeth, Or The Scent Of Smoke On Their Body And Hair— Help Them Give Up The Habit. All Of These Have The Potential To Worsen The Smoker's Addiction, Leading To Their Eventual Cessation. These Are A Few Of The Factors That Have Shown A Lot Of Smokers To Give Up. These Ten Harmful Effects Of Smoking That Occur On A Daily Basis Frequently Make Quitting Difficult.

1. The Stench Of Smoke Emanating From Them. Because Individuals Find The Smell Disagreeable, They Cannot Confuse The Smell Of Cigarettes With The Scent Of Regular Smoke, Nor Would They Characterize It As Pleasant. Some Individuals Find It So Annoying That They Actually Throw Up Upon Smelling It. Additionally, Smoking May Be Very Unlucky For The Individual Because Of

The Stigma Associated With Smoking In Society. People Tend To View Smokers As Evil Or Careless, Which Makes Others Avoid Them Because The Smell Of Smoke On Their Person Immediately Conjures Up These Negative Associations. Because They Face Discrimination From Others, Smokers Typically Have An Awareness Of The Smell Of Smoke On Their Bodies And Hair And Do Not Particularly Enjoy It. For The Majority Of Smokers, The Smell Of Their Breath Is A Specific Sensitivity. Numerous Individuals Who Have Dated Smokers Have Reported That It Was An Awful Experience, Akin To Making Love With Burnt Paper.

2. They Experience Changes In Taste And Scent. Not Only Does Smoking Make You Smell Like Smoke, But Smoking Also Dulls Your Senses. Taste And Smell Are Particularly Affected By Smoking, Making It Difficult For Smokers To Distinguish Between Different Kinds Of Scents. This Is Among The Ways Smoking Impairs Physical Well-Being. Smokers Frequently Question Why They

Can No Longer Taste Or Appreciate Some Items The Way They Once Did. The Reason For This Is That When Cigarette Smoke Enters A Smoker's Lips And Nose, It Changes Their Taste Buds And Perception Of Smell. Smokers Gradually Lose Their Senses As A Result Of This. Some Smokers Become Aware That Their Taste Preferences Have Changed And That Some Meals No Longer Taste The Same, But The Process Is So Slow That It Can Be Challenging Or Nearly Impossible To Notice. The Senses Quickly Return After Quitting, And The Smoker Realizes That He Has Been Slowly Murdering Himself In A Cage. When Smokers Give Up, Their Fantasies About Food Become Even More Dramatic, This Occurs Gradually Over Several Days And Can Last For Up To Three Or Six Months.

Making The Choice To Give Up Smoking

If you have been smoking for a long time, you may be wondering if there is a natural, healthy way to help you stop without becoming addicted or gaining weight. First and foremost, the most beneficial course of action is to quit. At the conclusion of this guide, you will be briefly introduced to the kind of advantages that would result from choosing to stop.

You will be required to respond to the following question in this : Why and how will you kick the habit of smoking? The most crucial question that we shall address in this compendium is that one.

In all honesty, this is the same issue that scholars and medical experts have been posing for years. A number of hypotheses purportedly explain the right timing for quitting smoking. This specific model is based on studies that demonstrate that smoking habits are likely to alter over time for an individual. As such, it recognizes that different people will inevitably stop at different rates. While some people may pick up the practice of quitting quickly, others may need more time. However, individuals who go at their own pace are often doing so in a healthy manner.

It would help if you examined the subsequent phases in order to comprehend this:

(1) The Pre-Contemplation Stage: During this phase, the smoker doesn't even entertain the idea of giving up. He continues to smoke for "enjoyment." It's not even anything he thinks is terrible at this point.

The second stage is the contemplation stage, during which the smoker is actively considering giving up the habit. It should be highlighted, though, that the smoker is not yet prepared to take any significant action to break the habit. "I think I'm ready to quit, but I'll have to think about it because I expect a lot of stress next week, and I'm not sure if I could handle it without a single cigarette stick," he would say.

Smokers who reach the third stage, preparation, are severe enough to contemplate giving up the habit. Due to prior attempts at quitting during the last 12 months, the timeframe is typically one month. They are typically the ones who were able to create a thorough plan for stopping.

(4) The Action Stage: Smokers have already taken a concrete step to break the habit at this point. This continues until the sixth month of quitting smoking.

(5) The Maintenance Stage: The newly quit smoker could encounter fresh difficulties after six months. At this point, the newly quitting smoker is actively making the required changes to kick the habit altogether. Usually, it entails incorporating other healthful behaviors that will end the addiction to nicotine and tobacco forever. In addition, further precautions are made to prevent specific, predictable outcomes, such as weight gain.

But keep in mind that the smoker alone has the authority to make this crucial choice. While several may contribute by pushing you to continue with your quit, only you have the ultimate power to make that huge commitment.

Once you are familiar with the phases, you must identify a valid cause for stopping. It needs to be captivating enough to hold your attention. You can make that crucial choice by asking yourself the following questions: *) Are you concerned that you smoke? If so, is it a result of the various illnesses that smoking might cause?

*) Do you really think that giving up smoking would be good for you? Do these advantages make you want to keep smoking less than ever? * Do you know of any examples in your community that demonstrate smoking can be fatal or cause significant health issues?

*) Do you possess the motivation to declare that you are prepared to give up smoking for good?

In order to proceed with creating your strategy, you must establish a deadline if you are genuinely considering resigning. You can go to the following phase with the aid of this. You can't just toss away your cigarettes and other associated items if you really want to break this bad habit. There's just no way to wish for the best. To successfully break the bad habit, you must prepare yourself enough and receive some outside encouragement.

Prior to proceeding to the following phase, you should give the following crucial topics further thought:

*) You ought to understand that smoking is a habit. It takes a more vigorous habit to unlearn. This will make it more straightforward to you why you ought to give up smoking.

*) It is important for smokers to realize that smoking is addicting. Even while this is common knowledge, many people are unaware of how much more difficult it is to stop. You will be prepared to make a complete attempt to stop when you have come to terms with the truth that you are struggling with addiction.

*) Throughout the procedure, you require all the assistance you can receive. This will support you when you want to give up already.

You are now prepared to go to the next phase. Once you've made that momentous decision, you can move forward with scheduling your resignation.

The Approach I've Taken To Stop

I've made numerous attempts to stop smoking, but I've never been successful. One rainy afternoon in October 2015, a few days after my birthday, I was coughing and sneezing a lot. After giving it some thought, I realized that part of the reason I felt sick was the withdrawal symptoms from cutting back on cigarettes. My daily smoking has decreased from twenty to five sticks.

I therefore gave up at that point and went through the most terrible withdrawal symptoms. However, I continued to try until February 2016, at which point I gave up completely once more. How did I succeed this time? Continue reading.

There are several ways to stop smoking, but I've only quit cold turkey, which means I stopped right away and didn't have any withdrawal symptoms since I had been getting ready to avoid them. I altered my diet for a month, eating more fruits, veggies, and dairy products (especially milk), which helped my body get rid of the withdrawal symptoms.

Dairy products, including milk, are known to impart an unpleasant flavor to smoke. In addition, I began training, lifted weights, worked out, and followed the "Post smoking plan" before quitting completely.

I enjoy not smoking the most because it allows me to do more. I regret every second I spent smoking, and those seven minutes are a waste.

I told myself that there would be no justifications, that nothing was hidden, and that all of the steps I took to stop smoking would be revealed as my technique of quitting. The most effective way to stop smoking is to just give up and not light another cigarette. I'll tell you, if you prepared your "post-smoking goal," you'll be alright. The only thing that matters in the fight against smoking is your decision to stop when and how to stop, which is more of a psychological fight than a physical one.

Since I'll tell you, that's when the good times start. You're going to have the greatest fun you've ever had, and before you know it, you've been imprisoned in this world of smoking, out of which very few people have survived. The fact is that by choosing not to light another cigarette, you are going to leave this world and no longer have to exist in it. Nothing more has to be mentioned because, as you are aware, the most of us have probably experienced withdrawal symptoms; this is both normal and anticipated.

The quick answer to the question "have I experienced any withdrawal symptoms?" is "no," and you'll probably wonder why. It's essentially because I followed my prescribed course of action, ate my recommended food, warmed up my body before extinguishing my final cigarette, and made an attempt to learn about and understand how my body would respond to quitting smoking.

The Causes

A few had to halt due to health issues. This is not unexpected, as diseases caused by tobacco claim the lives of nearly 400,000 Americans each year. The most prevalent illnesses that are directly brought on by smoking include ulcers, lung emphysema, bronchitis, malignancies, strokes, heart problems, and peripheral vascular diseases.

Furthermore, smoking may make treating pre-existing diseases more difficult. Smoking increases the risk of anesthesia and the consequences that follow surgery.

Another important reason to quit is social pressure. Many of the more than 50 million former smokers in our country still think smoking is unpleasant, smelly, and filthy. Although it used to be seen of as a refined habit, many of today's peers look down on those who smoke.

Some smokers now believe that they are looked down upon and lack self-control because they are too smart to give it up. Some want to give their children a better example by quitting smoking.

The cost of smoking is another important factor. Many recall saying, "I'll quit smoking cigarettes if they ever go up to $1 a pack! A couple who smokes could be

When they realized they were spending thousands of dollars a year to feed their addiction, they were inspired to stop. In addition, smokers leave burn marks on their cars, couches, clothes, and carpets. Not only might expensive burns occur, but unintentional fires could also develop. In reality, smoking cigarettes is the primary cause of nearly half of all fire deaths in our country.

Many people who had previously quit smoking for an extended length of time have since started smoking again. They reported feeling happier, calmer, and healthier after quitting smoking. But their inability to understand permitted them to lure a puff. Their full-fledged addiction was reinforced as a result.

Some people require assistance in giving up smoking. Despite being aware of the risks, calamities, and costs, they are unable to quit. Smoking cigarettes is an addiction. It's critical to keep in mind that addiction is a lifelong condition. It's not too hard to quit smoking when you give it up for a little while. Thoughts of smoking will cross your mind from time to time, but they won't compare to the withdrawal symptoms you'll experience in the early stages of quitting.

However, you have to continually remember that just one hit will return you to a completely dependent state. After then, you'll have to restart quitting smoking or give it up altogether. These are both disgusting choices. Think about them both if you're thinking about puffing. Adhere to the victorious and never take another puff!

What Smoking May Do To Your Conceptual Framework And Ability To Coexist Sexually.

Women who smoke may experience problems with their reproductive health. For example, women who smoke will undoubtedly have trouble getting pregnant. Additionally, smoking during pregnancy might lead to health issues that affect the mother and the unborn child. n which the developing organism enters the uterus outside of the uterus and endangers the mother's life.

• Problems pertaining to the placenta, the organ that connects a mother and her child. The placenta may separate from the uterus too quickly (placental unexpectedness) or be in an undesirable location (placenta previa). These problems may result in actual death, premature birth, early delivery, or other issues with the delivery, some of which may necessitate an emergency Cesarean section (C-segment).

• Early deliveries and stillbirths; • Late pregnancies and low birth weight babies;

- Having a child who has a congenital fissure in addition to possible congenital disabilities

Babies born to mothers who smoke both during and after their pregnancies are also more likely to die suddenly from SIDS.

Smoking takes away from the joy of being a mother.

In Males

Smoking damages veins throughout the body. One essential component of male erections is the bloodstream in the penis. Men who smoke are more likely to experience erectile dysfunction. The longer and more they smoke, the greater the risk.

Smoking can also have a detrimental effect on sperm quality, which can reduce its richness and raise the risk of miscarriage.

It is less enjoyable to smoke when in a fulfilling relationship.

Different ways that smoking affects your health

Smoking damages almost every organ in your body and has many other adverse effects on your health. Here are a few examples of different ways smoking might negatively impact your health:

increased risk of rheumatoid joint inflammation, increased risk of cataracts (blurring of the eye's focal points), and increased risk of age-related macular degeneration, which can cause visual impairment

- It takes longer for wounds to heal

Numerous illnesses linked to smoking might negatively impact one's quality of life. Diseases related to smoking can make it more difficult for you to breathe, move around, work, or have fun. Quitting smoking can reduce smoking-related disability, especially in younger smokers.

What smoking can harm children and teenagers?

Children and teenagers who use tobacco products or smoke cigarettes may develop health problems. In the long term, they can include the actual medical disorders discussed above, which can start at far younger ages.

Nicotine compulsion, which frequently leads to long-term tobacco use as youngsters, is arguably the most challenging problem. There's also some evidence that nicotine negatively impacts teenagers' mental health. It is essential to understand that the majority of e-cigarettes and similar products also contain nicotine.

Children and teenagers who smoke regularly will typically experience more health problems than children and teenagers who do not smoke. These problems may include: • Hacking spells; • Windedness, even when exercising; • Wheezing or heaving; • Continuous migraines; • Expanded mucus (body fluid); • Severe respiratory diseases; • Severe cold and influenza symptoms; • Decreased actual wellness; and • Helpless lung development and capacity, which increases the risk of COPD in the future.

According to some Smoking Statistics Worldwide, 6 trillion cigarettes are produced annually. That's enough to buy 1,000 cigarettes for each person on the planet. Six trillion cigarettes would fill the Empire State Building several times over, the Roman Colosseum several times over, and an entire football field piled a mile high. We can also think about the amount of cyanide, tar, and other synthetics that are inhaled when smoking. Every time you smoke a regular cigarette, 10 milligrams of tar enter your lungs. This means that annually, 60 million kilograms of tar are inhaled into the combined lungs of smokers.

Somewhat opinionated: 10,000 kg may fit inside a railroad freight car, which means that every year, 6,000 vehicles full of tobacco tar are inhaled by smokers worldwide.

• The fastest cigarette hand roller in the middle of the 1800s could produce about one cigarette per minute and about 1,500 cigarettes per day. Tobacco companies began investing in machines that would move cigarettes quickly—roughly 20,000 cigarettes per minute, to be exact—and operate nearly around the clock (this is a massive business that benefits the producers and kills you, the customer).

• One billion people smoke regularly, which translates to 1 in 7 people worldwide, lighting up every day.

*In 1900, the average smoker smoked 54 cigarettes a year; by 2010, that figure had risen to 1,500 smokes!

• In the United States, cellular breakdown in the lungs was virtually nonexistent before 1900. Still, in 2010, nearly 160,000 people died from cellular research in the lungs, accounting for 30% of all malignant growth deaths in the country.
• In the United States, hand-down cigarette smoke is responsible for 50,000 deaths annually.

Have a Plan for Quitting

Setting a date for your quit should be the first step in developing a plan to help you stop smoking. Give exact details regarding the day, month, year, and time. After that, on the day you decide to quit smoking, have one final, leisurely cigarette before discarding the rest.

Place every penny you saved on smokes into a glass jar.

You will be able to see how much you have been spending on cigarettes thanks to this. Then, utilize this cash to purchase an opulent purse or on a cruise. This money can also be used to buy stocks or real estate.

Grab a nutritious snack and take it with you.

Try healthy foods like celery sticks, carrot sticks, sunflower seeds, and nuts in place of smokes. When the impulse to smoke strikes, resist it by eating a carrot stick or a few macadamia nut pieces.

Play a computer game during your cigarette break instead of going outside.

What should you do during a smoke break now that you've given up smoking? You might, however, play any other computer game or solitaire in it instead. However, be sure the game you select isn't compulsive.

Make a smoke-free area in your house.

If you are the only smoker in your home, it can be challenging to quit. Thus, it's a good idea to prohibit smoking in your house. Let your guests know that your house is a no-smoking area when they are over. If necessary, hang a "no smoking" sign on your door.

Imagine yourself in a tennis match.

Experts say that one of the best ways to quit smoking is to picture yourself playing tennis or to really play the game. Thus, if the impulse strikes you to light up a cigarette. Shut your eyes and imagine yourself on a tennis court competing against professional players like Serena Williams and Roger Federer.

Make a routine change.

If you typically smoke straight after breakfast, consider switching things up and running errands or going for a walk instead.

Consider acupuncture.

A study done in Derby, Connecticut, found that acupuncture helped reduce cigarette smoking. So, schedule an appointment with your acupuncturist if you're finding it difficult to suppress your urge for nicotine. Tiny beads can also be taped to the acupuncture points. Squeeze the dots when the impulse to smoke arises.

Give up abruptly.

This is most likely the most effective smoking cessation method. All you need to do is make the decision never to smoke another cigarette again and stick to your word. Eighty percent of smokers who have successfully quit do so using the "cold turkey" approach, according to research.

Be in the company of encouraging individuals.

It's a good idea to surround yourself with people who will encourage you during the first few weeks. Avoid as much as possible the company of those who support your smoking habit.

Try the replacement therapy for nicotine.

Numerous individuals who have effectively stopped smoking make use of nicotine replacement therapy. Research indicates that using nicotine replacement medication can boost the likelihood of quitting smoking by 50% to 70%. You can experiment with a variety of nicotine replacement solutions, including:

Nicotine patches: These are sticky patches that you apply to your skin. For 12 weeks, you should wear one patch per day. Every morning, apply a patch on your arm or stomach. Every day, pick a different body part to prevent skin rashes.

This nicotine gum is appropriate for smokers who wear dentures. Eat or drink nothing for fifteen minutes before and after using the gum, and chew it three to four times. For a duration of 30 to 90 days, chew a piece of gum every two hours during the day.

Lozenges containing nicotine - Nicotine lozenges help smokers suffer fewer withdrawal symptoms. Just as your physician or therapist has instructed, take the nicotine lozenges. If you are nursing a baby or pregnant, do not use this.

Additionally, if you frequently get heart palpitations and chest pain, stay away from tablets.

Nicotine inhaler: You must inhale the nicotine through your mouth using this device, which looks like a cigarette. As instructed on the packaging, use the inhaler.

One of the best methods for managing withdrawal symptoms is nicotine mouth spray. It is advised that you apply the spray four times each hour for best results. Mist beneath your tongue. Avoid getting any rush on your lips. While using the nicotine spray, avoid eating or drinking anything.

THE HISTORY OF THE CIGARETTES

Smoking has been documented as early as 5000 BCE in a number of different cultures across the globe. Tobacco was initially used in religious rites as a sacrifice to the gods, a purifying sacrament, or a way to change the consciousness of priests and shamans for the sake of enlightenment or divination. With the discovery and colonization of the Americas by Europeans, tobacco consumption spread quickly throughout the world. In nations like India and Sub-Saharan Africa, where smoking was already familiar, it blended in (primarily with cannabis). It brought with it a new way of socializing and using drugs in Europe.

Throughout history and civilizations, smoking has been viewed as a cure-all and a deadly health risk, as well as holy and immoral, sophisticated and vulgar. Public opinion began to change enormously against smoking in the later decade of the 20th century, especially in the West.

On the other hand, it was widely known at the beginning of the twenty-first century that tobacco was highly addictive and ranked among the world's top causes of disease and death.

This number was estimated to have increased to over 5,000,000 in 2003, then to 6,000 in 2011, and by 2030, it was expected to reach 8,000 every year. Roughly 80 percent of those fatalities would occur in developing countries, according to estimates. Although smoking rates were declining in a number of nations in Western Europe, North America, and Australia,

Quitting Smoking's Impact on Reproductive Health

Prior to attempting to conceive, women should give up smoking as soon as feasible. However, quitting smoking at any point throughout pregnancy can benefit the health of both the mother and the unborn child.

It is preferable to treat or prevent small-for-gestational age in a fetus that occurs before or early in pregnancy. It reduces the possibility of having a child that is underweight for its birth weight. The best defense against nicotine's harmful effects on a growing baby is to stop smoking before becoming pregnant. Premature birth can be reduced by adopting preventative measures before getting pregnant and during the first trimester of pregnancy.

Why It's Difficult to Smoke

Smoking makes you a social outcast in our culture more and more. When you take a cigarette out of your pocket or ask for a lighter, people nearly look at you like you're a monster.

Smoking is not permitted in bars. Generally speaking, smoking is not allowed in hotels. You can't smoke in your apartment complex, and you most likely won't be able to smoke inside your own house anytime soon.

As if the shame in public and unclean looks weren't enough, smoking causes your body to break down, one cell at a time. It could be fatal to your health; it killed several of my family members. The "beauty" of smoking is the multitude of ways it can influence one's well-being. It is the underlying cause of cardiac issues, lung cancer, hypertension, and even erectile dysfunction. Smoking, in contrast to a professional boxer, isn't scared to punch you below the belt.

Everybody has heard tales of a friend of a friend who smoked a pack a day and lived to be one hundred and ten. However, let's quit deceiving one another and ourselves;

we all know that's the exception rather than the rule. We know there is a link between smoking cigarettes and poor health, even though the tobacco firms have spent billions of dollars trying to deny it.

If you're reading this book, you probably already know that smoking has a harmful impact on your health, and that's only the beginning.

Smoking also leaves you smelling horrible. The smoker is the only one who is unaware of how offensive their smoke is to others. It wasn't until I put down my cigarette that morning and looked into my daughter's scared eyes that I started to notice how awful my belongings smelled. It only affects your breath at first. Next is what you're wearing. Also, all of your clothes will smell like a smoker's clothing after a prolonged period of smoking.

If you've ever gone to purchase a secondhand car, you can immediately detect whether the seller is attempting to conceal the car's previous owner as a smoker. But even with all the deodorizers, incense, sprays, and chemicals they use to cover it up, you can still smell it, and it bothers you. We finally leave every place we smoke smelling horrible, and we take that awful scent with us everywhere we go. Restaurants used to have separate areas for smokers and non-smokers when I was younger. There was no partition between the two regions; it seemed as though the air wouldn't mix. It can be unpleasant to eat when the person smoking behind you is doing so. As a result, our culture has changed. We've increased cigarette pricing in several states and tightened regulations on where it's acceptable to smoke as a result of growing awareness of the health risks associated with smoking. Nowadays, smoking is prohibited in the majority of public areas.

Lastly, and perhaps most significantly, smoking can make one feel helpless. "I could quit smoking whenever I feel like it" is a joint statement. I choose not to. But then that instant arrives. When you make the initial decision, "You know what? I have no desire to smoke. I'm going to take a brief break from it, and you find that you can't. You understand that it's not going to be easy to get rid of this monster that's poisoning you and giving you a foul odor.

The worst sensation of all is the sense of helplessness. It feels as though you have lost control over your actions, emotions, fate, and conduct. That could be harmful.

Benefits And Drawbacks Of Smoking

Burning anything and breathing in the smoke allows the drug to taste and enter the bloodstream. This is known as smoking. The ten benefits and drawbacks of smoking are listed in this article.

Worldwide, smoking is a prevalent habit among people. Worldwide, there are about 1.3 billion smokers.

One of the most popular ways that people consume drugs recreationally is by smoking. The most commonly smoked plant is tobacco. In several cultures, smoking is not just a leisure activity but also an integral component of ceremonies. Some people think that smoking can lead to spiritual enlightenment.

Smoking, when done appropriately with the right herbs, can have several health benefits. These herbs are not as bad for a smoker's health as smoking tobacco cigarettes.

Indian tobacco, called Lobelia, is an excellent aid in quitting smoking. With the exception of being less addictive and having no adverse side effects, it is nearly identical to nicotine. Peppermint is another herb that smokes without containing nicotine.

The benefits of smoking are rarely mentioned because it is one of the leading causes of illness and death. However, they still exist.

It's claimed that smoking cigarettes dramatically lowers stress and improves relaxation, focus, and mental toughness. It has antidepressant properties as well. It is among the primary causes of smokers' refusal to stop. They believe that if they quit, the pressure from their families and jobs would be too much for them to bear. When faced with difficult circumstances, smokers may turn to cigarettes to help them relax and make decisions. Cigarettes cloud their lungs, but they have brighter thoughts.

Among the best ways to manage hypertension is to smoke. Resulting in a reduction in blood pressure. Consequently, the likelihood of acquiring chronically high blood pressure is minimal to nonexistent. Cigarette smoking can reduce your chance of getting this illness by roughly 30%.

One effective strategy to lower the risk of obesity is to smoke cigarettes. Cigarette producers advertised cigarettes as a "great way to lose weight" in order to sell their products to ladies in the 1920s. However, this does not imply that smoking is the only way to reduce weight. Nicotine is thought to help people manage their weight by decreasing their hunger and appetite.

Taking a smoke breaks the ice. For other people, smoking is a social gathering place with pals. It's possible to view smoking as a "requirement" to fit in with your friends. Consequently, some smokers find it simpler to identify with a group. For them to blend in, they must smoke.

Smoking dramatically reduces or manages diseases like Parkinson's. Studies show that smokers have a far lower incidence of Parkinson's disease than nonsmokers. The nicotine found in cigarettes is the cause of this impact. For smokers, smoking lowers their chance of Parkinson's disease by 41%.

Smoking undoubtedly causes a lot more problems than it does health advantages. One of the leading causes of premature death is smoking. T

Nicotine impairs taste and smell perception. It alters taste receptors, causing people to lose their sense of taste and, as a result, become less hungry and find bland food.

Pregnancy is more challenging for female smokers. They also have an increased chance of early labor and miscarriage.

Smoking has an impact on a person's exterior appearance in addition to their internal systems. Tobacco smoke clings to hair and clothing. If someone has recently smoked or been around someone who smokes, you can tell right away. Additionally, smoking can raise the risk of infections or inflammations that cause teeth to turn yellow.

On the other hand, tooth and bone loss are the drawbacks. Smokers' fingertips and fingernails are stained when they handle cigarettes.

In smokers, bronchitis is more common. Nonsmokers who are exposed can also be impacted, particularly young people. Smoking aggravates airways and is a contributing factor to chronic coughs, sometimes referred to as "smoker's cough."

The A. R. A. R. method for quitting smoking in 30 days.

A combined team of clinical psychologists and social therapists led by Jeff Auckman conducted an innovative study of smoking addiction in men and women between the ages of 18 and 70 in 30 countries, including China, New Zealand, Iran, South Africa, Western Europe, and the United States of America. The result was the A. R. A. R. system, which was developed as recently as 2016. Years of test trials and meticulous research preceded this development.

These four essential elements—A = Accept, R = Respond, A = Act, and R =

React—have been found to be crucial for accelerating the reversal of cigarette smoking patterns and reducing addiction in smokers who are both proven people with a substance use disorder and casual users. Every step builds upon the one before it, forming a chronology and set of maps that may be used to guide and track a person's degree of commitment and desire to stop smoking. As we get started, we'll provide you a summary of these processes that you can quickly understand without sacrificing the message's quality, and we'll also make sure the main point is kept front and center interestingly and straightforwardly.

No one dies from smoking. To be honest, it doesn't. Again, it does not. Any idea for that?Sounds fantastic. Whoa! I see a thousand arrows of incredulity directed right at me. I know you are thinking about the remark above a lot, subtly producing a ton of numbers, volumes of facts, and figures you must have accumulated over the years, all in anticipation of a potential barrage of counterarguments against me. I can picture you now, recalling images and different details from books, research papers, statistics, government-commissioned reports, and news articles you must have read and taken in bits and pieces over the years. Words and phrases you are probably familiar with, like "lungs," "untreatable sick," "died from smoking," "cancer," "complications," "life expectancy," and "tobacco," would be flashing through your mind like police lights at a crime scene. Additionally, you should definitely double-check the sentence to make sure you understood it correctly. It is still there, indeed. Remember to understand. People do not die from smoking. To what extent is that true? Stay put.

A Few Useful Reminders

Firstly, finish your shopping list.

Straws for the Emphysema Breathing Technique and as NLP anchors: both a coffee stir and a straw

This water bottle with the visible straw is utilized to remove toxins and nicotine from your system, as well as to hydrate and serve as an NLP anchor.

Lollipops are used to control blood sugar levels and provide oral fixation.

Sugar packets: If you think you need a little extra sugar to keep your blood sugar from falling too low or to avoid cravings.

Apple juice increases acetylcholine and blood sugar levels.

You feel calmer with the aid of lemon balm extract. It is referred to as a natural valium.

The ability of cinnamon oil extract to regulate blood sugar is well-known.

2. Practice breathing with straws.

3. Read the material, get your blood boiling, and remember to use rage to stop yourself from relapsing. The tobacco firms are steadily poisoning you as they amass wealth and claim that your illness or death is predictable. Give them the finger or say, "Screw you," and vow never to purchase this product again.

4. Become knowledgeable. Find out how many distinct harmful substances can be found in cigarette smoke: There are about 4,000 different forms of cancer that smoking is linked to. How much time does

each cigarette's carbon monoxide stay in the air?

6. Control your blood sugar levels to ward off cravings

7. As a hand-to-mouth tool, use lollipops to control your blood sugar levels and to keep you from overindulging and gaining weight after you stop.

8. Look after yourself and ask for assistance from others when necessary.

9. Inform everyone that you are giving up smoking and ask them to support you in not smoking around you. Take this seriously, or be available for a conversation if necessary.

10. Use the money you save and your increased self-worth to treat yourself to something exceptional.

The secret to success is preparing ahead of time on how to satisfy your cravings:
Completing a meal. As soon as possible, get up from the table, engage in a fun activity, brush your teeth, and apply mouthwash. Walk or pick up a new pastime.

Consuming coffee. Modify everything about your coffee-drinking experience, even the location and mug you used to smoke. Save your morning coffee for when you go to work. Make use of the nondominant hand.

Conversing over the phone. When you are at home, use a phone in a different room. There might be little you can do to move locations at the office. While you are on the phone, keep tiny objects close at hand for handling.

In between jobs. Before starting your next project, consider going for a little stroll, reading a of a book you're enjoying, or even smoking a cigarette.

Following a disagreement, setback, or unfortunate incident. If you're still agitated or furious, take a little stroll around the building to release some steam.

In a vehicle. Cars are becoming a popular place to smoke because so many employers have outlawed smoking. Please take out the ashtray from your car and replace it with potpourri or small pieces of paper with your reasons for quitting smoking inscribed on them. Sing along to your favorite song on the stereo or turn on a book on CD while you drive instead of smoking.

Social gatherings and activities at work can spark the temptation to smoke. Here are some ideas on how to stay away from these:

Additional smokers: Steer clear of the smoking locations at work. Choose a different entrance, arrive at work at a time when the smokers won't be there, or be aggressive with them if there is a door where people who smoke congregate before or during breaks.

During work breaks, stay away from areas where smokers congregate. Seek out the companionship of nonsmokers, and spend your holiday walking with them.

People: Your social life may suffer if you give up smoking. You don't have to stay away from parties entirely, but if you do go, don't go outdoors with your pals to smoke. Try to sit or stand as far away from people who are smoking as you can if the party is outside or if people are smoking indoors. If you need to, go out and get some fresh air, but please don't smoke!

Alcohol: Your determination to abstain from smoking may wane after a drink. When you initially quit smoking, you can decide to stop drinking alcohol entirely or to drink less of it. Changing the type of alcohol you drink and where you consume it might help you avoid triggers, but it won't assist with your weaker will.

What You Get From Smoking

There are numerous detrimental effects of smoking on the body. It is, in fact, one of the leading causes of avoidable deaths worldwide. For instance, in England, each year, 80,000 people, or one in two smokers, pass away from smoking-related illnesses.

What Are the Health Effects of Smoking?

Smoking has an impact on every bodily part. Maybe you would give up when you realized how bad it was.

A smoker's heart is affected.

It harms the heart and blood circulation, increasing the risk of peripheral vascular disease, cerebrovascular disease, heart attack, and coronary heart disease, among other illnesses.

The heart beats more quickly than it should because of the nicotine in cigarettes and tobacco, as well as the carbon monoxide that is released when smoking. They also raise the possibility of blood clots. The coronary artery lining is harmed and furred by the additional chemicals in cigarette smoke.

The risk of a heart attack is doubled by smoking. That means that the risk of dying from coronary heart disease is twice as high for smokers as for non-smokers. Thankfully, there is still hope for you. Your chance of contracting this disease and dying from it is halved if you give up smoking for a year. If you give up smoking for fifteen years, this danger goes away entirely.

Smoking impairs blood flow.

When you smoke, the tar in cigarettes and other tobacco products enters your bloodstream. It contains toxic ingredients that can thicken and increase the clotting potential of your blood. In addition, it narrows your arteries and lowers the quantity of oxygen that reaches your organs, raising your blood pressure and heart rate.

Smoking has digestive effects.

You run the chance of developing stomach cancer or ulcers if you smoke. The muscle that regulates the esophagus or the lower portion of the gullet is weakened by smoking. Additionally, it permits stomach acids to flow in the incorrect direction, which results in reflux.

The likelihood of developing kidney cancer increases with the frequency of smoking. Researchers have found that the risk of kidney cancer is 1.5 times higher in individuals who smoke ten cigarettes a day than in nonsmokers. This chance doubles if you smoke at least twenty cigarettes a day.

Skin is impacted by smoking.

It lowers the amount of oxygen that reaches your skin. Therefore, if you smoke, your skin is likely to age more quickly than that of non-smokers. Additionally, your risk of developing cellulite increases.

Furthermore, smoking causes premature skin aging. Smokers appear ten to twenty years older than their peers for this reason. Additionally, the likelihood of creases around their mouth and eyes is three times higher. They also frequently have sallow, yellowish-gray complexions and sunken cheeks.

Smoking has an impact on bones.

The result is weakening and fragile bones. Brittle bones are more common in women smokers than in anyone else.

The brain is impacted by smoking.

It raises the risk of stroke for you. Actually, it makes you fifty percent more likely to get hurt. This, in turn, may result in death or severe brain damage.

Because smoking weakens the blood vessel wall, it also raises the risk of brain aneurysm. There is a chance that subarachnoid hemorrhage will happen if this wall ruptures. This type of stroke has the potential to cause both death and brain damage.

The lungs suffer from smoking.

Smoking has been linked to colds, coughing, wheezing, and asthma. Additionally, it can result in deadly illnesses like emphysema, lung cancer, and pneumonia. Actually, it accounts for 83% of fatalities from lung cancer and 84% of deaths from chronic obstructive pulmonary disease.

Smoking has an impact on the mouth and throat.

It results in issues like gum disease, foul breath, discolored teeth, and impaired taste buds. Worse, it raises the chance of developing cancer in the tongue, voice box, gullet, lips, and throat. Indeed, it is the cause of over 93% of oropharyngeal malignancies.

Reproduction and fertility are impacted by smoking.

Men may experience impotence as a result of it damaging the blood arteries that supply blood to the penis. It can also harm sperm, lower the number of sperm, and induce testicular cancer.

Similarly, smoking can lower a woman's fertility. A study found that smokers are three times more likely than non-smokers to have trouble getting pregnant. It may take them almost a year to become pregnant. Furthermore, smoking raises the danger of developing cervical cancer.

Smokers are less able to recover from HPV infections, which frequently result in cancer. Smokers during pregnancy also run the risk of miscarriage, stillbirth, sickness, and early delivery.

Are You Stressed?

Learning and regularly practicing self-hypnosis has the added benefit of reducing symptoms associated with stress and boosting immune system activity. Managing daily issues related to our work, relationships, and general living conditions causes a significant amount of stress in our lives.

The same problems that many individuals face on a daily basis include living in a noisy area, being stuck in traffic on their way to work, not getting along with coworkers, worrying about debt, and having to wait in lengthy lines. Taken one by one, these inconveniences might seem like little more than annoyances. They have the potential to be very stressful over time.

Significant life transitions, such as divorce, losing one's job, a spouse or family member passing away, or suffering a severe disease or handicap, are the most stressful situations.

Even happy occasions can occasionally include stressful elements. A woman might receive a raise and more prestige, for instance, but she might also experience stress from managing colleagues who are now her subordinates.

Both winning the lottery and finding out you've unexpectedly inherited a sizable amount of money are happy occasions that cause tension.

Although most people view being married as a happy event, there can be stress involved in organizing the wedding, choosing who to invite, and handling relatives.

Inadequate stress management might result in significant issues. Chronic stress exposure has been linked to psychological and physical ailments such as anxiety disorders and heart disease.

Regular self-hypnosis practice can help lessen the symptoms of stress.

The Reaction to Stress

One of the pioneers in the research of stress response was the Canadian scientist Hans Selye. During his time as a medical student in the 1930s, Selye observed that patients with seemingly unrelated conditions had many of the same symptoms, such as apathy, weight loss, and muscle weakness. Selye thought that these signs could be a normal reaction of the body to stress.

Selye investigated how lab rats responded to a range of physical stresses, including extremes of temperature, poisoning, intense physical activity, and electric shock.

He discovered that his lab rats responded similarly to each of the many stimuli. The thymus gland, a gland involved in the immunological response, shrank in Selye's rats, and the rats developed abnormally large adrenal glands and bleeding stomach ulcers.

Medical professionals increasingly recognize that stress has a role in a number of different health issues. These issues include hypertension, heart disease, cancer, problems with chronic pain, and numerous other medical conditions.

A person's body experiences several changes that increase both physiological and emotional arousal when they perceive an event to be stressful.

First, the autonomic nervous system's sympathetic division is triggered.

Pupils enlarge, respiration quickens, and sweat production rises.

The fight-or-flight response is another name for this response. The body is getting ready to fight the threat or run away from it.

Long-term stress causes the body to become chronically hyperactive, which leads to resistance failing and weariness setting in.

The body is susceptible to illness and possibly death under this condition. The immune system is a marvel of perfection on most days. It seeks out and eliminates external invaders like viruses and bacteria to shield your body from illness. Nonetheless, there is strong evidence that stress inhibits immune system function, making you more vulnerable to infectious infections.

A compromised immune system also makes it more difficult for an organism to regulate naturally existing mutant cells, which overproliferate and eventually cause cancer. Smoking exacerbates the situation because each puff increases the amount of poisons and carcinogens in your body, increasing your susceptibility to disease.

If you follow the advice in this book, you will become more at ease. One of the most valuable lessons you can acquire is this one. You'll relapse-proof yourself and become a nonsmoker effortlessly when you're at ease.

Drugs and Additional Therapies To Encourage Smoking Condition

When correctly applied, medications can assist you in quitting smoking. The various nicotine replacement therapies have significantly reduced nicotine levels and can alleviate withdrawal symptoms and headaches that may occur when quitting smoking.

Non-pharmacological prescription drugs can also assist you in reducing your cravings for nicotine.

Your doctor or nurse can also assist you in deciding whether or not such medications can benefit you. Additionally, your doctor can determine whether using both non-nicotine and nicotine replacement drugs will help you more.

Once you have a conversation with your healthcare provider, make sure you inquire about the appropriate methods of using the medication. Based on studies, many smokers do not take their medications as prescribed. It won't work well enough for you if you don't use these medications correctly.

The information sheet provided by your physician will specify the proper method for administering the medication.

Necessary Replacement Education

You cannot use these medications if you continue to smoke or use other tobacco products. Combining nicotine with other drugs can be harmful, so you should completely stop smoking before beginning to take nicotine replacement therapy. The treatment typically lasts between two and three months. Even though you can always buy these products without a prescription, consult your doctor first to find the most appropriate medication for you.

NICOTINE Patch: Purchasing a NICOTINE patch does not require a prescription from your doctor. These patches typically have different strengths.

There are brands available in 5, 10, or 15 mg strengths, as well as those with 7, 14, or 21 mg strengths. Make sure you read the product packaging carefully to understand the strength, based on your smoking amount, that you have.

ü Nicotine gum, also known as chewing gum, has already assisted many people who have wanted to give up smoking for the past 20 years.

The gums or loafers can be purchased at pharmacies without a prescription. Follow the instructions and make the correct use of the gum or lozenges.

üNicholine Spray: To purchase this spray, you must have your doctor's prescription.

ü Nicotine Inhaler: This is a type of vapor or mist that you will inhale into your mouth and upper chest.

Non-Native English Practise Medicines

Bupropion hydrochloride, a medication intended to treat depression, has been found to assist those who wish to stop smoking. It comes in several brand names, but it is also available in generic form. A relatively new medication that can assist smokers in breaking their habit is phenylephrine.

Seek guidance from your physician to determine which of these medications can help you with your smoking cessation.

Smoking And Suffering The Repercussions

The human body reacts negatively to smoking because smoke, in any form, is bad for your health.

It may surprise you to learn that the only product that is promoted and actually causes cancer is cigarettes.

The idea that cutting back on filtered cigarettes has no negative consequences is entirely false. Additionally, smoking one to four cigarettes a day has serious side effects that increase the risk of dying young.

The risks are the same whether a person inhales a high-tar, low-tar, or high-nicotine brand. You smoke more than you usually do because these are the safer options.

The person frequently takes shorter butt-length hits more regularly, but the damage is still the same. Consequently, the amount of the addictive substance, nicotine, which is intoxicating, does not change.

Research demonstrates that smokers with low tar or nicotine levels do not have a decreased risk of developing lung cancer. Small doses of nicotine are harmful to the brain and central nervous system, causing pleasurable sensations that lift the smoker's spirits and fuel their desire to smoke more.

As a result, the person develops an absolute addiction to this unhealthy habit, which causes physical withdrawal symptoms when the person tries to kick it.

A person experiences jitteriness and restlessness as a direct result of quitting smoking when they lose the peace and tranquility that smoking artificially produces.

Advantages of Giving Up Smoking

There are several excellent benefits of quitting smoking that have been discovered over time, and this information is backed up by research on people who have given up the habit. After just twenty minutes of quitting smoking, the rate drops.

Twelve hours after stopping smoking, the CO level returns to its usual level.

After two to three weeks of quitting smoking, the respiratory system performs much better, and blood circulation improves.

Primarily, Diseases like coughing, which is exacerbated by smoking, can be brought on by smoking.

Smoking contributes to an increase in respiratory disease severity. Another illness that is highly associated with smoking is respiratory illness. It has been determined that prolonged smoking causes even a traditional person's breathing to shorten. It has been noted that these physical disorders take one to nine months to resolve after quitting smoking. However, there might be a noticeable improvement.

Symptoms of Withdrawal

Smoking implies that nicotine, similar to heroin or cocaine, is highly induced in the body. Destroys not only the body's physical components but also the link's psychological components. Thus, the mere notion of giving up smoking could have a negative psychological impact. Making one feel compelled to keep going rather than give up.

It is impossible to resist the unwelcome and unavoidable pressure from friends and coworkers.

If you are determined enough to control yourself and resist being drawn into such a deep relationship, you become aware of your future. Therefore, you should first seek to be persuaded of the reasons for giving up smoking. We usually say that the decision to resign.

The symptoms include lightheadedness and lethargy during the initial days.

You might also experience awkward fatigue.

This might be the result of heavy tobacco use.

Mental Depression: Nicotine has a charming effect that helps you feel better.

Anger and impatience: Nicotine affects not just the lungs but also the blood vessels, brain, hormone system, and metabolism (metabolism). Consequently, the effect of withdrawal may create discord throughout your entire body, placing further strain on your mind.

In this cutthroat world, tension, stress, and stress are your constant companions.

Sleeping and focusing may be your body's response to hormonal imbalances. You sense a loss of harmony because your mind needs to be in proportion to sleep soundly and concentrate on any task that requires your full attention. Additional Digestion and Appetite Problem

Physicians have found that quitting smoking frequently has paradoxical effects, such as altered appetite and digestion. Indigestion may result from the mental strain brought on by not smoking a cigarette. In certain other instances, it has been demonstrated that the cessation of nicotine has a direct effect on metabolism, causing the person to become more hungry.

In humans, nicotine addiction inevitably has some psychological effects. The report states that there is insufficient evidence to conclude that nicotine has a psychological impact on humans, despite evidence of nicotine addiction and possible underlying neurobiological mechanisms in animals. Moreover, research on smokers provides a large portion of the psychological effects of nicotine on humans. This raises the question of how much of the psychological effects of smoking itself are attributable to smoking.

How to Give Up Smoking After Giving Up, You've been able to take the first step toward stopping smoking because of an unquenchable passion. Being able to swim against the tide makes you one of the luckiest people on the planet. To stand out from the crowd and demonstrate a strong sense of determination, you should reach out to your family and friends. Is there any way you could lose that position even if you were able to answer the most crucial call of your life? Is there anything that can rival his fortitude? Would he even attempt to embarrass himself in front of his family members? How do you present yourself to your kids? He is prone to forgetfulness and indecision. Alternatively, you could demonstrate that smoking is so valuable that no one can give it up. Your spouse and kids should always come first. Consider you. Lastly, we have nothing to say to you if you choose to assume the risk of losing your standing in the family and society. But suppose you decide to stick with the more noble course of action. In that case, we can support you to the fullest extent possible, and this will significantly assist you in achieving your desired but unconventional objective. You might notice that you are drawn to people and situations once more since smoking puts your body and mind under the influence of nicotine. Use an iron grip to restrain these unwanted mental urges, as one more mistake could return you to where you were even years later.

The most enormous void in the modern world is awareness. During a sexual relationship, people are unaware of their partner's feelings. Adolescents do not realize that mental blue movie watching leads to recovery. The risks and perils of being in an unknown location in an unexpected environment are unknown to the surveillance team. The physical and psychological damage that drug addiction causes to the younger generation is not known to them. When you took your first puff, you might not have known about the consequences of smoking. He now understands the dangers of tobacco.

You need to be aware of the probable circumstances that will cause a relapse because you have already demonstrated the first step toward maturity by giving up smoking. We may have come upon some general dominant ideas or triggering incidents. The smoking-prone mind becomes more active by observing the people smoking around them. So start you need to avoid smoking areas. Thanks to the government for hiring organizations to maintain a separate smoking area.

The Record Of Cigarette Smoking

Did you understand that tobacco is indigenous just to the continent of The United States and Canada? It's believed by many that cigarette-smoking tobacco was presented to the Europeans by Columbus, who discovered the method from Indigenous Americans.

Furthermore, considering that the smoke from some plants offered hallucinogenic encounters, these as well were no questions utilized to raise the spiritual meeting.

The commercial approach passed the hand-rolled entry numbers in the mid-1980s, and today, kretek controls approximately 90 %

of the Indonesian cigarette market. Manufacturing is among the most significant incomes for the Indonesian federal government. Also, the manufacturing, which is expanded on some 500 independent makers, utilizes some 180,000 individuals directly and over 10 million indirectly.

Marijuana cigarette smoking in India has actually been understood at the very least given that 2000 BC and also was initially discussed in the Atharvaveda, which goes back a couple of centuries BC.

What does all of this point to?

These days, we undoubtedly understand a great deal more about the Earth, the planetary system, and even our bodies. We are aware of a lot of risks that earlier generations were unaware of when it comes to our nutrition and overall health.

Wikipedia has provided us with a comprehensive history of cigarette smoking. Still, it is essential for anyone perusing the material to remember that just because a method has been used for centuries does not mean that the risks associated with it aren't real. It's straightforward to argue, "Well, people have smoked for centuries, so what exactly is the harm?"

Cigarette smoking must coexist with modern scientific research, medicine, and our increased understanding of our bodies. These things should give us the "upper hand" in determining whether a particular method is healthy and balanced and, if not, to what extent.

The following credible eyewitness report of tobacco cigarette smoking is from 1617 and is written by a Spanish agent; nevertheless, by then, the practice had been thoroughly embedded in Persian culture. By utilizing many of the everyday items used to release aroma for tobacco cigarette smoking, the practice of smoking cigarettes evolved as part of the Japanese tea event.

By the time European settlers arrived in the Americas in the late 15th century, tobacco cigarettes were widely used as a recreational activity. Before tobacco became widely available, smoking marijuana-infused cigarettes was standard in the Centre East. It was also an everyday social activity that revolved around the hookah, a type of water pipeline. Mainly after tobacco was introduced, smoking became a significant aspect of Muslim society and culture. It was also ingrained in rituals such as marriage celebrations and funerals, and it was represented in poetry, literature, clothing, and other works of art.

Let's examine that subject in relation to cigarette smoking.

Many prehistoric people practiced many of the things that we have learned in the past, such as bloodletting and human sacrifice. Columbus wanted to establish sail because he wanted to confirm that the world had not been standardized, as many of his peers believed.

Using Self-Awareness And Mindfulness To Help You Stop Smoking

The final of this e-book will cover the last three all-natural ways to help people stop smoking. These three are self-awareness, mindfulness, and hypnosis.

Entrance

By definition, hypnosis is a changed level of consciousness that gives the impression that the subject is asleep or in a trance. Typically, this approach is utilized to address a few medical and psychological issues. It can be used, for instance, to teach someone how to manage their discomfort. It can also be used to treat other ailments, such as weight problems, speech problems, and, in this case, addiction.

During hypnosis, a person appears to be unconscious, but in reality, they are not. Contrary to what magicians and stage actors may tell you, a person in hypnosis cannot be forced to do anything against their will; they are nonetheless conscious of their surroundings.

In a hypnosis session, you can be made to consider or visualize all the harmful effects of smoking in order to cure your addiction to smoking. One of the most well-liked methods of hypnosis to quit smoking is the so-called Speigel Method. The three tenets of the approach are as follows: (1) smoking is poisonous to the body; (2) your body must survive for you to survive; and (3) you only have one body; therefore, cherish and take care of it while you still have it. When a smoker feels the temptation to smoke, they can be taught the technique of self-hypnosis, in which they repeat to themselves all the negative aspects of smoking and the positive aspects of quitting.

The effectiveness of hypnosis in treating smoking addiction is a topic of much discussion. Still, hypnosis offers hope to a great deal of people in addition to its other advantages. If you would like to employ this technique to stop your smoking addiction, you might want to get in touch with a nearby hypnotist.

Being alert

You must be able to experience and notice everything about smoking in order to employ mindfulness to support your stopping efforts. It will be simpler to concentrate and find the drive to continue when you are attentive to what you are doing. Consider this: when you light a cigarette, you are urged to taste it, feel the cigarette between your fingers, smell it, and watch as the tip burns. You are also encouraged to inhale and exhale to feel the smoke enter your lungs. Now, once you've smoked, pay attention to your breathing, your hair, and how you think. And taste your mouth from the inside out. Keeping all of these in mind, you will be able to understand the precise effects of smoking and what it does to your body and health. You lack the understanding necessary to take a firmer stance against quitting.

Being mindful encourages one to become aware of their surroundings. Spend some time observing the ordinary senses that you take for granted, such as the ability to smell the fresh air, touch the hands of others, hear people laughing, taste a delicious meal, and even see the smiles of those you love. Engaging in these activities can help you realize the value of your body. Above all, though, remember that life is the greatest thing there is, and you should never take any actions that could endanger it.

Self-knowledge

Self-awareness is crucial for anyone trying to give up smoking. This is likely the process's most vital component. Being able to recognize your unique personality, character, and originality is the first step toward becoming self-aware. According to a new study, smokers who are self-aware find it simpler to give up. Your chances of successfully quitting smoking and other unhealthy habits increase with the awareness you have of your own needs and desires.

Knowing when to quit doing something that is unhealthy for you should be extremely straightforward if you have a clear idea of what you want to accomplish in the near future and what your goals are. While the effects of smoking might not be recognized or experienced right away, you will undoubtedly regret it in the long term. You don't want to be the person who is known for having died from a smoking-related ailment, do you? That wouldn't present a positive impression of you or set an excellent example for your loved ones.

There are several herbal products and natural medications that you can take that have been shown to help people stop smoking, but nothing is more realistic than making the change within. Think positively and be aware of your objectives. To get over a challenge like this addiction and move closer to your goals, you have to have confidence in your abilities and strengths. You have to always believe in yourself before you can help others and have faith in yourself. You need to realize that you are doing this for your family and yourself. One thing to be concerned about during an addiction detox is relapse. However, if you are sure that you will never travel that route again, you shouldn't be afraid. Never. /

Additional Easy Methods To Help You Beat The Need For Nicotine

Try the following methods to lessen your need on nicotine:

Acupilla

Although smoking cigarettes instantly makes you feel more relaxed, the long-term impacts are far worse. If you smoke, you light up a cigarette to relieve stress or take a break from work, but there's a safer method to unwind and get rid of worry. Because acupuncture has a calming impact on the body's nerve system, it minimises the need for nicotine and the symptoms associated with withdrawal. Beta-endorphin is released during an acupuncture treatment, and this helps you physically stop smoking.

In order to treat nicotine addiction, acupuncture primarily uses disposable needles inserted into the palm, wrist, and ear. For speedy results, a little electric current is occasionally utilised. The first week will require three 30-minute sessions, while the second week will require two sessions. After two or three months, you could occasionally need a few follow-up appointments. Additionally, acupuncture will assist in clearing your bloodstream of harmful substances like tar and nicotine residue.

Your breathing will return to normal, your coughing will stop, and your digestion will become better.

One thing to keep in mind is that while acupuncture can lessen your urge for nicotine, it cannot alter your habit. Your willpower becomes vital at this point because only you have the power to change your behaviour. If you are accustomed to smoking at stressful or emotional times, going without a cigarette will make you feel exposed and alone. If smoking has been a long-standing habit for you, it will take some time to break the habit. Family and friends must be there for you during this challenging withdrawal period.

Vapour cigarettes

According to a study in "The Cochrane Library," smokers who use e-cigarettes to quit are more likely to cut back or give up smoking altogether. A third of smokers were able to reduce their smoking, and 10% were successful in stopping altogether, according to the research. Co-author of the report Professor Peter Hajek advised using e-cigarettes for smokers who have not been able to successfully quit using nicotine patches. Empirical data suggests that long-term smokers who switched to e-cigarettes were able to stop smoking. Keep in mind that the FDA has not yet approved e-cigarettes. Although some e-cigarettes contain nicotine, they are not as hazardous as traditional cigarettes.

Reflection

You can overcome your addiction to nicotine by practising meditation. 60% of the smokers in the study, according to University of Wisconsin researchers, were able to successfully stop smoking by utilising meditation. You can control your cravings, stress, and bad feelings throughout the nicotine withdrawal phase by practising meditation. If you follow a nutritious diet and engage in regular exercise, meditation will be beneficial. By strengthening your mind and assisting with the control of nicotine cravings and external and internal triggers, meditation can help you completely quit smoking. Select meditation if you wish to stop smoking and live a healthier life; it will have no negative effects and offer you great health benefits.

Eat less to stop smoking

Diet becomes crucial when trying to stop smoking in order to maintain your smoke-free status. Before smoking, have milk, fresh fruits, or vegetables like carrots or celery. When you smoke after consuming these items, you will taste something bitter, which will assist you in quitting smoking. Eat fruits high in vitamin C, such as guava, oranges, and lemons, to help curb your cravings for smokes. Nicotine makes up for your body's lack of vitamin C, so if you have enough of it, you won't feel the need to smoke as much. To quell the temptation to smoke whenever it arises, consume some salty snacks like chips or pickles. The aroma of dried fruits can also help reduce your desire to smoke. To cut down on smoking, keep your mouth occupied with sugar-free candies or chewing gum. Steer clear of alcohol, coffee, and red meat as these will make you crave nicotine more.

magnetic fields for quitting tobacco

According to studies presented at the 2013 Neuroscience conference, TMS, or transcranial magnetic stimulation, can reverse the brain's addiction to nicotine. The pre-frontal cortex and the insular cortex, two areas of the brain linked to nicotine addiction, were the focus of a thirteen-day study including 115 smokers. Researchers discovered that the capacity to overcome addiction is enhanced when magnetic fields are applied to specific regions of the frontal lobe. In order to produce reliable findings, this method is still in the development stage and requires additional research.

Low-powered laser treatment (LLLT)

Low-level laser therapy, or LLLT treatment, is beneficial in reducing pain, inflammation, and the healing of wounds. For smokers, LLLT relieves pain by releasing endorphins, a chemical that is produced naturally. In order to treat nicotine addiction, endorphins regulate the body's energy levels and mimic the effects of nicotine on the brain. This is a painless, non-invasive, chemical-free way to help you kick your nicotine addiction. We're still testing this strategy, so it might not be effective for all smokers. If you decide to use this method, make sure it works first because some of the gadgets are just light-emitting diodes, or LEDs, designed to deceive people.

Select the approach you believe will work best for you, and if you don't get results right away, don't give up.

6: A Few Pointers to Help You Remain Smoke-Free, Avoid Gaining Weight, and Handle Stress After Quitting

Use these pointers to avoid smoking.

▢ You'll have a difficult time the first few days, so avoid smoking in places like churches, theatres, malls, museums, restaurants, and libraries.

Make sure to stay hydrated to sustain a nutritious diet and get seven to eight hours of sleep per night.

- If you feel like you should be holding something else in your hand instead of a cigarette, try holding a pencil, paper clip, or coin.

Make a new routine to keep yourself occupied.

If you are in a difficult circumstance in life and you feel that smoking may help, remember why you gave up smoking. Don't forget to consider your family when making decisions. Consider their assistance in helping you stop smoking as well as the consequences of starting up again.

To feel refreshed, wash your teeth if you are tempted to smoke.

Whenever you experience the temptation to smoke, get assistance by talking to a friend or contacting a stop-smoking hotline.

Consume five to six meals daily to maintain stable blood sugar levels and a healthy energy level. This will lessen the craving for nicotine.

Take a bath or a shower to help you ignore the impulse to smoke.

To prevent nicotine addiction, try a widely used method. Wear a rubber band around your wrist, and snap the band to remind yourself not to smoke even one cigarette whenever you get the impulse to smoke.

Time to Give Up

Sometimes, Alex told his mother, "I just smoke." She was a wellness fanatic, and he needed to comfort her, telling her to calm down. I'm not dependent on it. I'm free to stop whenever I need to."

You should strive to avoid harming your body and your life by quitting smoking if you have studied one of this book carefully. Maybe, like Alex, you expected to cease sooner or later. You haven't stopped, though. Maybe you've tried, but you felt that it was too much trouble.

A Difficult Habit to Break

"Most current smokers don't smoke because they need to (above and beyond 50% say they wish they had never begun), but because they are addicted," writes Phyllis Balch in her book Remedy for Dietary Recuperating.

Why is stopping such a difficult task? Why is smoking such an allure?

Some people seem to find that smoking helps them relax when under stress. Besides, who in today's world wouldn't benefit from a little pressure relief? In any event, keep in mind that nicotine functions more as an energizer than a relaxing. Your brain first receives a burst of dopamine, the "vibe great" chemical, and as a result, you experience a temporary decrease in anxiety. You come alive again when you're nervous. The more smoke you take, the more

Unfortunately, your body becomes resistant to nicotine very quickly, so you need more and more to get the desired effect. When you're hooked, you may become reliant not only on the apparent relaxation and stress relief, but also on the flavour, aroma, and feel of a cigarette in your mouth and in your hands. You may even get addicted on the lifestyle that surrounds your habit. Some people find it impossible to quit smoking when they go for their daily workouts.

In a recent Brain Science publication, Jessica Grogan, PhD, hypothesises that smoking causes momentary relaxation because of many associated propensities rather than the cigarettes themselves. Even when you take an hourly break to go smoke, for example, it's possible that this is only a way for the break to relieve some of your stress. Studies have indicated that if you truly eliminate the tendency completely, your level of anxiety would decrease much more.

Of course, an enslavement also means that when you stop smoking, you'll experience withdrawal symptoms. Who expects to handle irritability, defeated mindsets, headaches, difficulty focusing, fury, anxiety, jitters, and cravings for nicotine? Obviously, no one does. It's possible that your fear of stopping has prevented you from stopping.

Okay, so you made it clear that you are a target. No one is berating you. It's intriguing, for sure, but only for those who've smoked. Right now, the query is: How would you stop?

You Could Try. various substances

Treatment for nicotine substitution (NRT) entails gradually weaning off of cigarettes and substituting various forms of nicotine. The problem with these alternatives is that, according to the American Cancer Society (ACS), all of them carry the potential for side effects, and some of them may even end up being just as addictive as cigarettes. If you decide to try NRT, be sure you use the appropriate dosage; too much nicotine can have real side effects, even passing. Remember that NRT addresses physical dependence; therefore, the ACS also recommends using a different programme in addition to NRT to address psychological dependence. The five acceptable forms of NRT recognised by the ACS are the fix, biting gum, nasal splash, inhalers, and capsules.

A few prescription drugs from doctors are also available. But, should you decide to pursue this course, you'll need to collaborate closely with your PCP due to potential side effects, some of which may not be humorous.

Isn't it time to address electronic cigarettes? While some have found success with these newly developed devices in helping people give up actual cigarettes, most experts agree that it is too soon to say whether or not these can be used safely by everyone. These battery-operated replacements for cigarettes use a liquid that is broken down and then inhaled to simulate tobacco smoke. In addition to nicotine, the liquid contains additional dangerous synthetics and can be poisonous to children and animals.

The Toughest Way To Give Up: Health Issues

Three simple homework assignments are due this week: be yourself, have fun, observe, and ahh. And the most straightforward approach to stop smoking has been demonstrated for you: just be and then accept whatever arises in your being. This is the cornerstone of the simple smoking cessation method. Yes, it seems too simple.

Okay, because it is expected of us, let's now examine the problematic route. In order to accomplish this, we must first drive our bus past the assisted living facility, then the hospital, and lastly, the hospice. Oddly enough, most smokers believe they should start in this neighborhood when they are about to give up.

Nine times out of ten, the first response I get from a new class on the first evening is,

"Health reasons," which explains why they all want to stop smoking. Naturally, each participant in the class has their own unique personal health reason(s), but most of them quickly concur that "health reasons" are the leading causes of quitting. It makes sense in this case.

Concerned about the long-term effects of smoking on their health, even young, healthy individuals without serious illnesses express a desire to give up. They are able to sense its products, and they don't feel well.

The majority of elderly smokers have firsthand knowledge of the short- and long-term physical impacts of smoking. In the event that they lack such a firsthand encounter, their physicians will caution them about the negative consequences, the media will constantly remind them, and their relatives will persistently remind them of this knowledge.

Not to be forgotten (how can we?), the Surgeon General has recently added new warnings to every pack of cigarettes, stating that they are just as addictive as heroin or cocaine, that they can cause deadly lung disease, cancer, strokes, and heart disease, that they can harm unborn children as well, and that giving up smoking will significantly lower the risks to one's health. (Obviously.)

After a 25-year wait, all the cautions that the majority of smokers were mentally reciting are now present on the cigarette packets. It was inevitable that more explicit and comprehensive health warnings would appear on cigarettes eventually. These warnings will be helpful in encouraging smokers to give up, or more directly, they will prevent young children from duplicating the harmful weed experiments. That is advantageous.

It goes without saying that I am not disputing the hundreds of years of evidence proving smoking's harmful effects on health.

Centuries, indeed! King James was among the numerous early voices highlighting the dangers of smoking on one's health as early as 1604. Since then, similar cautions have been issued by other credible agents in every nation and century, despite the current trend of pretending that we were unaware of the health risks when we were children. The empirical data opposing smoking has only just started to make a dent in the strong social and economic momentum that the tobacco industry has enjoyed. (Yes, of course, when they were children, hospitals still had designated "smoking rooms." We had a designated smoking place just outside the gym at my high school.)

Over the past century, much scientific research has provided indisputable facts demonstrating the health risks associated with tobacco use.

Here are two further intriguing smoking-related health statistics that aren't often discussed in the media:

Actually, studies indicate that most smokers perceive smoking to have more hazards than non-smokers!

2. Despite the fact that smokers perceive a higher danger of long-term harm from smoking than non-smokers, the majority of smokers also secretly believe that they will be more likely to avoid these adverse effects.

It goes without saying that millions of smokers have given up due to health concerns. Not a dispute.

When he learned that I was a stop-smoking coach, an old acquaintance blurted out, "You want to quit? I'll tell you how to quit." "Just let your heart give out. Hear feathers of angels. That's what I experienced. In an instant, I went from eating three packs a day to none at all.

For some, that is a viable approach. This is how it has repeatedly occurred. Furthermore, not everyone needs something as terrible as a heart attack. Perhaps it's just a minor case of bronchitis, a flu episode, or sinus issues, but for some reason, at that moment and in that location, these minor health issues are enough to make these people realize they are more than just smokers and enable them to declare, "that's it, I'm done."

However, a lot of people are like my client, a construction worker who is currently unemployed due to health issues, who told me, "You know, I've already had three heart attacks." You would think I'd get the lesson. However, I still can't get rid of these dumb objects.

Individuals awaiting an organ transplant must abstain from smoking for a minimum of six months, and in certain situations (such as a replacement heart), they must refrain from smoking for an entire year before being added to the waiting list! This goes beyond simple anti-tobacco bias. It is based on case studies from actual life. The doctors were shocked that following a successful operation, ex-smokers with a new heart would begin smoking again six or eight months later!)One of my clients was giving up to go on the "heart transplant" waiting list. "I'm going to start smoking again one year after I get my new heart," she informed me.

One of the most heartbreaking and perplexing instances I've ever dealt with included a sweet little older woman who had previously received the devastating diagnosis of lung cancer—the main fear shared by all smokers. She underwent numerous surgeries and chemotherapy sessions, ultimately managing to reverse the diagnosis. The doctors had declared that she had clear lungs.

Unfortunately, she returned to smoking. After about a year, the doctors discovered new spots on her lungs and made an appointment for her to have further chemotherapy. She said to me, "Well, I don't start chemo until Thursday, so maybe I'll make Wednesday night my quit date," the last time she visited my office on a Monday morning. Wednesday evening? How come?

A medical background, fresh lung lesions, and chemotherapy on Thursday! One would believe she had struck the proverbial gold mine in terms of health hazard motivation if facing immediate health hazards—the close possibility of death!—were an adequate motivator. However, my elderly buddy decided she could wait until Wednesday evening. (The beloved woman had chemo-related issues, ended up in the hospital, and died that weekend.)

Indeed, a lot of people do give up right away when they receive a bad prognosis. The United States' smoking rates have decreased by about 40% ten years after the historic 1964 Surgeon General reported on the dangers of smoking, thanks to higher cigarette taxes and educational initiatives.

But over the past ten years, smoking rates have drastically decreased and, in some places, have even begun to rise again for some demographics. It seems that dread of potential health risks—that is, fear of dying soon—is an ineffective motivation. Have we all not had friends or family who continue to smoke despite being compelled to live with oxygen tubes taped to their noses?

How come?

To put it simply and readily, none of us ever truly feel like a statistic, even in spite of the data that highlight the risks associated with smoking. Conversely, though. Every one of us perceives oneself as a living, sometimes mystical, obviously multidimensional, and frequently enigmatic entity. Indeed, it goes without saying that we desire to follow our health and avoid our unhealthy habits. And for the most part, we're not too bad at it. The majority of us only go ice climbing in our tennis shoes, drive 95 miles per hour with using a seat belt, or sniff airplane glue.

While there are exceptions, seasons, and explanations for those exceptions, the majority of us do not limit our lives to the sole goal of maintaining our physical well-being. Health issues are typically just one small band of color in a rainbow of worries because there is so much going on in our lives right now—money, work, family relationships, household demands, social and political uncertainties, television, movies, the internet, the dog needs to be walked, and barbarians are at the door.

Naturally, our health suddenly or progressively becomes a greater and greater concern when it begins to deteriorate or when we encounter an unexpected issue. However, smoking itself reduces to a single hue—possibly a flashing red—across the entire spectrum.

It's interesting to note that despite the fact that a significant number of my clients have made their health concerns—chronic pain, a severe illness, COPD, emphysema, etc.—their smoking is still seen as a minor side effect of a much bigger problem.

Despite how politically correct these concerns may be, the issue with using "health concerns" as a reason to stop smoking is that it depends on the threat or actual occurrence of illness or death to motivate us to stop. Furthermore, we typically don't think clearly, aren't content with what we're doing, aren't at peace, or feel comfortable in our current situation when we're ill, on the verge of death, or extremely afraid. In this state, the decisions we make are usually quite flimsy and weak.

Thus, it will be helpful to review the Gallup poll results here, which indicate that behavioral changes are typically the result of people wanting to feel better about themselves and not feeling pressured by others or health issues.

Furthermore, it could be helpful to keep in mind Plato's observation that "the greatest hindrance in life is attention to health." Although Plato's viewpoint may seem a little absurd, even radical, nevertheless

Your positive outlook will get you through to the first day and beyond. Day Two
Look recognisable? Yes. A full day without smoking. You've probably done this before. The first three days are said to be the most difficult.

Given that you've been here before, day two is the hardest. What happens next? Just keep making the decision not to smoke! You have 48 hours left, and then you can go for home!

You were presumably fighting your subconscious minute by minute yesterday. Today won't be any different, but try to increase the time between your decisions to give up smoking. Try shifting the decision-making process from minute-by-minute to hour-by-hour. "SELF, I made it that last hour," tell yourself. After an additional hour, let's decide where to go.

After that, carry on doing that every 24 to 48 hours.

In addition, yesterday was more of a let's get by day. Recognise what I mean? This is the day that the actual work starts. Make breathing your first priority right now. Not just because your breathing will become better as your body returns to its original, smoke-free state, but also because your body might need to be more sure what that original state is. Your body may begin to feel apprehensive about making slight adjustments because it believes that nicotine obtained via the intake of tobacco smoke is its normal state.

How do you handle experiencing anxiety? Inhale. Breathing deeply, precisely! This one, we're going to tackle it like a Karate Kid. "In through nose, out through mouth," as Mr. Miyagi once stated. Inhale slowly and mindfully. Remember to maintain a straight back. It can be done while lying down, sitting, or standing. Repeat the process twice. Spend ten minutes on it. whatever the duration.

Bring positive energy and thoughts with you as you take a breath. Let go of your worries and negativity as you exhale. This is something you can practice all day, and in fact, for the rest of your life, anytime bad energy tries to overcome you.

This is also the first step towards mental quietness. I need a clear head. God forbid! But if you take a few minutes each day to pay attention to your energy and breathing, you'll find that it's a great way to address your primary source of stress, which is now quitting smoking. What are you going to do now that you've decided not to smoke today and realise that smoking actually reduced a lot of your stress? Yes! Sure enough! Inhale!

So for today, concentrate on quitting smoking right now, at this hour. When you get there, take care of the next hour.

Take deep breaths to de-stress in between.

As you finish the second day, you should be really proud of yourself.

Just make it through tomorrow, and you'll be on the motorway without smoking.

Day Three

Best wishes! It's day three for you! You haven't had a smoke in 48 hours! It's evident to you what this signifies. It implies that if you have survived these past two days, you are the only thing preventing yourself from going on.

Consider that for a moment. The incredible ability to select what you do is yours. You keep not smoking now. It is easy, but it's also tricky. Go past it!

Proceed with your hourly recommitment to abstain from smoking today. Utilize the minor triumph of quitting smoking every hour to gain momentum.

I read a book by Blair Singer titled "Sales Dogs," in which he talks to salespeople about a few essential and fundamental tools and mindset principles. "Celebrate All Wins" is one of those small tools that can grow into a significant tool and significantly alter your mindset. You succeed every hour you avoid smoking. Spend a few period alone yourself, clench your right hand into a fist, bring it in close to your side, and utter something like, "Yes!" or "That's right, nicotine, you got nothing on me!" One more hour in your absence! What possess you? Nothing at all! What's that?

Talking trash to your addiction can indeed help you quit smoking. If you get too into it, you could end up embarrassed, but honestly, who cares? You're enjoying yourself, and you're not smoking.

Appreciate the life you are giving yourself and the self-assurance you are instilling in your day-to-day activities. It's a significant accomplishment, and you ought to be proud of yourself. It's a lot of work, and you should be proud of yourself for choosing to stop and remaining stopped.

Moreover, you should set aside some time to express your thanks for today and every day going forward. This will be a difficult journey for you, and completing this mission will take the inner strength you already possess. I mentioned earlier that you should work for something bigger than yourself. This is a terrific time to be thankful for all the resources you naturally have to complete this task—you don't even need to believe in God.

It's also a good idea to start planning a little bit ahead of time today. Pause! How come? How come? Remain still! Now, wait a moment! I had assumed that we would remain "in the now." We are, but I want you to picture and consider what a year from now will look like. I haven't smoked for nearly three days. You're capable of doing this. You have already done it, and you are doing it now. You can carry on doing it in a year. Therefore, you might as well begin acting as though this moment—of quitting smoking—has already arrived. Say it aloud and proudly, please.

1: Quit Smoking Strategies Basics

Overview

There are a few fundamental things regarding stop-smoking resolutions that you should be aware of. You will discover the various integrated aspects of this remedy to assist you in effectively quitting smoking.

Why Is QuEttlngtK So Difficult?

However, if you smoke, you are aware that breaking the habit is easier said than done. You can assign blame to nicotine, a highly addictive tobacco product that can cause physical and emotional withdrawal.

But now that 2018 has arrived, this is the ideal moment to work on your cessation of smoking. You don't have to be discouraged if you still have trouble picking up your butt because you are not the only person who engages in this battle. Actually, there are actually a lot of people that make this one of the top 5 New Year's resolutions every year, so you are not alone in having the same problem as you. It would help if you dealt with your addiction and the associated habits before doing anything else.

Advanced Arrangement
It is one or more of the reasons that have led you to make this decision. This motivation needs to be reinforced by a strong and firm willpower in order to succeed. Examine your schedule and determine the ideal stress-free month for you to start. This will take some time to complete, but if you set aside a month, you can permanently kick your smoking habit.

Form a Support Group: You'll need to deal with withdrawal symptoms so that things will be challenging for the first several weeks. You can enlist the help of your friends, family, and coworkers. These individuals can serve as the ideal source of inspiration and resilience throughout these difficult times. You can also become a part of a support group.

Eliminate the Temptations
You need to identify the things that make you more likely to smoke. Steer clear of situations that could prompt you to go for a cigarette and extend the amount of time you spend hanging out with others who smoke. Clear your environment of cigarettes, as well as other smoking-related paraphernalia and equipment.

Engage in Physical Activities: Engaging in physical activities can assist you in resisting the impulse to smoke cigarettes whenever it arises. Take a walk in the park or visit the gym when you have plenty of free time.

View an Expert
You might also consult a behavioral therapist who can assist you with cigarette smoking cessation, or you could see your doctor, who can provide prescription

medications that can help with withdrawal symptoms.

Never Give Up: Just like with other addictions, quitting smoking is never simple. You must cease searching for opportunities in order to obtain a passport once more. Perseverance is essential. Even if there can be setbacks, use this as an opportunity to make your commitment more meaningful and challenging.

Take Notes From Past Attempts

Overview

As time passes, experience is always the best teacher. If you consider quitting smoking to be only tricky, remember your past attempts at quitting, and you will undoubtedly be encouraged to try harder than before.

Nobody Told Me That Quitting is Easy.

It can be challenging to achieve perfectionism. Many people even attempt repeated attempts, mainly since nicotine is one medication that can be highly addictive and difficult to avoid. That being said, you should never give up trying just because you weren't successful in the past.

Remember your previous attempts at stopping—what worked and what didn't. If one approach doesn't work, don't be afraid to try another one. You can learn something new every time you try. As you are all aware, this may already be the ideal moment that you will be taking a break for good!

Obstacles to Smoking Condition

Many people continue to smoke either because they believe that the habit helps them in some way or because they are afraid of the ill effects that they could experience if they start. Among the most prevalent concerns are the ones listed below:

The necessity of smoking for stress relief: There are still plenty of healthy and effective methods, such as exercise and meditation, that can help you relax and are beneficial to your entire body.

The fear of depression: Quitting smoking can generally make a person feel a lot better about themselves and entirely in control. Particular support is available for individuals suffering from mental illnesses or who were previously diagnosed with a mental disease.

The dread of gaining weight: The ideal approach is to focus on how you feel and appear physically instead of focusing on your weight. Numerous other methods can assist you in maintaining your weight.

The fear of withdrawal: It is well known that nicotine is an addictive substance with unpleasant withdrawal symptoms. However, they are only temporary symptoms, and the use of corrective medication will lessen the effects.

Prepare ahead of time and adjust routines.

After learning from your past mistakes, it's crucial that you properly prepare yourself for the one day you're planning to make a favorable impression. Think about your surroundings and the items that require alteration. Eliminate everything related to tobacco products, along with other things such as furniture, cars, and work spaces.

Never allow others to smoke when you are in their vicinity. Try to ask them not to use tobacco products when you are close by or place cigarettes and similar tobacco products in areas where they are visible to you.

If you've tried quitting before and failed, consider altering your routine. Make use of a completely distinct route when heading to work. Keep your brack in a different location. Take actions that will alleviate your stress. Another thing you might try is distracting yourself every time you feel the need to smoke or use tobacco. Talk to others, take a stroll, read a book, or engage in physical activity.

Resuming breathing exercises is the first step in quitting smoking. It's okay to overcomplicate in order to succeed; this method is simple, practical, and will improve our ability to breathe. You smoke less the more you live.

If you smoke, especially if you smoke a lot of cigarettes every day, you are also limiting the quantity of air and, most importantly, oxygen that you bring into your body on a daily basis.

In actuality, each time you inhale while smoking, you are simultaneously bringing smoke and air into your lungs. For this reason, it is simple to comprehend that, with each inhalation, you are bringing in a small amount of air, particularly oxygen, which you must then multiply by each puff of smoke you take throughout the day.

More than food and water, oxygen is our primary fuel and is necessary for every metabolic function in our bodies. Therefore, smoking a cigarette won't make you more energetic; on the contrary, it will make you less productive than you could be if it doesn't worsen your metabolism.

If you don't believe me, try doing a strenuous physical activity just after quitting smoking. You'll find that it's much more complicated because your blood hasn't been adequately oxygenated before. You'll be breathing soon and clutching your knees or hips with your hands.

Because it has more to do with the quality of your life than your health, this factor is frequently overlooked.

Steps to take? It's actually straightforward: all you need to do is start breathing pure, fresh air again, just like we all did when we were first born and for many years afterward. When we were first born, we learned how to breathe.

Take a few hours of free time; ideally, you should travel to a park, the countryside, the seaside, or any other place where you may be in close proximity to nature. Then, start breathing and experience the rush of breathing in fresh air and oxygen. Feel the air as it enters your nostrils, travels through your throat, and finally reaches your lungs.

Fill them as full as you can, naturally, and hold the air for a short while to feel the charge energy retained. Visualise the air being released, together with the oxygen, throughout your entire body. When you reach the top, release your breath and give yourself up entirely. You are renewing your own life. Energy is oxygen.

You will find, after doing this easy exercise, that there are much more benefits to inhaling clean air than drawbacks.

Now, you may go on to a much more comprehensive workout that you can perform every day to boost your metabolism and have more energy: circular breathing.

Four phases make up the fundamental process of circular breathing: 1) Breathe in from your nose.

2) Suck in air through your lungs.

3) Breathe out via your mouth; 4) Pause till your lungs are empty, then repeat step 1.

The success of this exercise is due to the fact then often we are not aware of breathing not rightly, may be too rapid, or you may make a short apnea. So we employ a two-step sequence inhale-exhale

When we do not, we recognise that we do not hold the air for enough time to take the proper quantity of oxygen.

Instead, following the stages of the circular breathing, you can breathe in an effective method. The duration of each phase might be vary from person to person, generally it lasts 3-5 seconds, but you have to try and discover your rhythm. You will find it after a few breathes. You can manage the amount of repetitions by yourself, as you feel more comfortable. You can do so even just once for a fast surge of energy. However, you must not, under any circumstances, force the breathing, and you have to stop breathing only if you feel uncomfortable throughout the workout.

Start breathing correctly is a habit that is excellent for everyone, not only for smokers, everyone can gain power and energy. The next time you want a cigarette, or rather a cigarette desire you, instead take a big breath, this is the best thing you can do and it is incredibly inexpensive, it costs you nothing!

We have begun to breathe again; now, we have to imagine ourself differently; we have to master the following method, visualising...

www.ingramcontent.com/pod-product-compliance
Lightning Source LLC
Chambersburg PA
CBHW052151110526
44591CB00012B/1938